Date: 12/6/21

BR 388.32 MUR
Murray, Julie,
Delivery drivers /

Delivery Drivers

Julie Murray

Abdo Kids Junior
is an Imprint of Abdo Kids
abdobooks.com

Abdo

MY COMMUNITY: JOBS

Kids

abdobooks.com

Published by Abdo Kids, a division of ABDO, P.O. Box 398166, Minneapolis, Minnesota 55439.
Copyright © 2021 by Abdo Consulting Group, Inc. International copyrights reserved in all countries.
No part of this book may be reproduced in any form without written permission from the publisher.
Abdo Kids Junior™ is a trademark and logo of Abdo Kids.

Printed in the United States of America, North Mankato, Minnesota.

102020

012021

THIS BOOK CONTAINS
RECYCLED MATERIALS

Photo Credits: Alamy, iStock, Shutterstock

Production Contributors: Teddy Borth, Jennie Forsberg, Grace Hansen

Design Contributors: Candice Keimig, Dorothy Toth

Library of Congress Control Number: 2020910588
Publisher's Cataloging-in-Publication Data

Names: Murray, Julie, author.

Title: Delivery drivers / by Julie Murray

Description: Minneapolis, Minnesota : Abdo Kids, 2021 | Series: My community: jobs | Includes online
    resources and index.

Identifiers: ISBN 9781098205805 (lib. bdg.) | ISBN 9781098206369 (ebook) | ISBN 9781098206642
    (Read-to-Me ebook)

Subjects: LCSH: Truck drivers--Juvenile literature. | Delivery of goods--Juvenile literature. | Community
    life--Juvenile literature. | Occupations--Juvenile literature. | Cities and towns--Juvenile literature.

Classification: DDC 388.32--dc23

Table of Contents

Delivery Drivers

Delivery drivers bring things from one place to another.

They use cars and vans.

They also use big trucks!

Worldwide Services
Synchronizing the world of commerce

MICHIGAN
C71176
24

7

They use GPS. This helps them with directions.

9

Alex is a driver.

He delivers food.

Mary delivers the mail.

She puts it in the box.

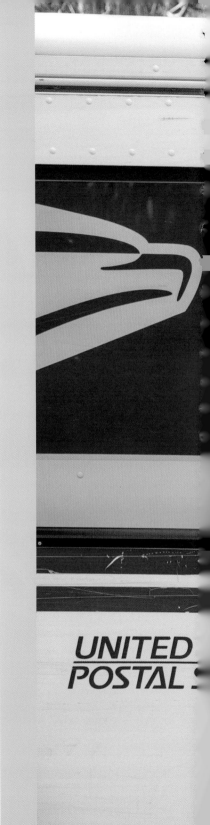

UNITED
POSTAL

STATES
ERVICE

13

Ada delivers groceries.

STAY HOME
WE DELIVER

Get the app.

15

Leo delivers a package.

He leaves it by the door.

Max delivers heavy boxes.

He uses a dolly.

Luke delivers flowers.

They make Kim smile.

A Delivery Driver's Tools

dolly

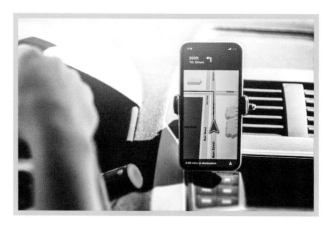
GPS

scanner

vehicle

Glossary

dolly
a low cart with small wheels used for moving heavy objects.

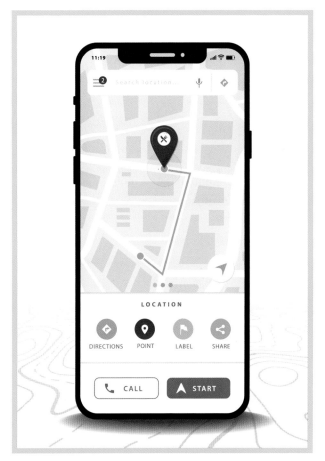

GPS
short for Global Positioning System, a satellite system that can pinpoint locations and give directions.

Index

Abdo Kids ONLINE
FREE! ONLINE MULTIMEDIA RESOURCES

Visit **abdokids.com** to access crafts, games, videos, and more!

Use Abdo Kids code

MDK5805

or scan this QR code!